BLOG SECRETS

E UNDERGROUND PLAYBOO

FOR CREATING STEADY CONTENT AND

OFITABLE INCOME STREAMS IN ANY NIC

AYOL HOP

Disclaimer

KAYOL R. HOPE

Helping small business owners find,

connect, and gain new paying customers

from the web.

Visit: www.kayolhope.com

WHAT'S INSIDE...

STARTING A BLOG

I've always enjoyed developing websites and started learning HTML scripting language from the age of about 12 years old. This was a turning point to developing niche sites and blogs for generating residual income and quick profit through flipping these starter businesses. Fortunately you don't need to know how to code (although it can help) due to the ease-of-use of web technologies such as Wordpress or Shopify that are very affordable.

When I state very affordable I truly mean it as blogging for me has become one of my first steady streams of income online. At this point the $5-10 each month is laughable considering that each site or blog makes substantially more revenue than what it cost to run making each one a valuable asset.

When it comes to starting a blog you can base it around an Evergreen online business niche as these tend to generate steady income for the long term with less competition and lower investment risk.

Some examples of the best Evergreen niches are:

* Health
* Financial
* Relationships

None of these are ever going away anytime soon as people are always seeking help with health be it weight loss, looking good or feeling good. Even though many people are always seeking wealth and financial freedom. Plenty of scammers have given the industry a bad reputation especially in the Make Money Online or Network Marketing, there are still plenty of legit ways to profit online. Lastly, people constantly seek advice when it comes to relationships and dating.

There is more topics and various ways to tackle these subjects with in a single site or blog just ripe for the taking. All you need is a genuine interest or passion for a niche because everyone has a unique voice and writing style to attract the right target audience of like minded people. If you choose a niche you know nothing about or aren't excited about than you will find it a chore to write consistent content instead of being motivated and driven to do so which will become apparent to your growing audience.

The other type of blog you can start is based around a trend which is typically a popular product or subject that has garnered mass media attention. This can be very profitable if your quick to take advantage but usually lead to short term gain.

I believe starting a blog around a product or service rather than a niche market limits a webmaster or blogger. When Fidget Spinners where at the high of popularity I repurposed a copy of one of my existing websites in my portfolio by quickly swapping out a few changes and adding a relevant domain name (website name such as kayolhope.com).

The domain name investment was around $10 while the listing cost on an online auction marketplace was another $25 investment. It sold as a starter website for $170 providing me over $100 in return after taxes and fees. not Bad for $35 and 20 minutes or less of work. Rinse and repeat that process 5 days a week or in your spare time and you can easily generate an extra $1000 a month or more on top of any other passive income method or regular 9-5 job.

My web hosting provider plan allows me to host an unlimited amount of websites or blogs for under $10 per month which I use and highly recommend

Hostgator - http://kayolhope.com/hostgator

Too many marketers focus on investing in domains in the hopes of turning a quick profit when with a bit more development could yield a much higher value as a business-in-a-box solution. It is kinda like harvesting crops before they fully bare fruit. What a waste.

Most web hosting providers include a Wordpress or a 1-click-installer to setup a blog for your site automatically and just start writing and publishing content. You can use one of the many free themes or invest in a premium theme if you wish to give your site or blog the right look. To be honest your content should speak for itself and unless a specific feature in a theme is required than a premium is an optional investment.

I personally find that compared to Shopify stores that having a hosted site or blog using Wordpress gives much more control and flexibility while keeping investment costs to a minimum. This means that if the site changes ownership my margins are better due to less ongoing maintenance costs and I actually own the site or blog because it on a platform controlled by someone else other than myself. If I want to change the theme I have plenty of options including having everything top to bottom customized. Plugins for features can be easily added and removed as well.

WRITING
CONTENT

If "Content is King" than "Consistency is Key" and publishing posts each day on a relevant subject of your niche that others are searching for that is over 1000 words is ideal. It may take some time for search engines to find and index your content but on average once you have around 30 quality posts for a relevant category in your niche than you should start to see some positive results. On average this typically takes a good 35 weeks. Be patient as many times I'll publish an article and get discouraged since it isn't getting the results I desire and forget it by going on to the next thing to discover interest picked up in it around a month later.

Don't write too often or you'll get burnt out and search engines may not determine it as organic. By the same token don't handle more niches than you can at any given time. I'm comfortable and feel I have the resources to handle around 6-12 niche sites or blogs at any given time while 1-2 may be the best focus for someone else.

If you want to really grow an audience for your niche than repurpose the content for social media, video, and audio format for podcasts and be everywhere yet easily accessible that your audience is.

MONETIZATION

Set expectations right from the start. While slowly starting to roll out processes for generating income across your website or blog over time is one strategy many implement, I find it can turn off some of your growing audience so you might as well set expectations and lose the freebie seeker mentality by placing ads on your website or blog from the beginning.Why shouldn't you be compensated for providing valuable content and recommending the right product or services as a solution for your audience?

When you have a niche website or blog you don't just have that as an asset but all the affiliate commissions, your own products be it physical or digital related to the niche, but income from the ad revenue as well.

Try out different ad revenue networks as many of them pay better than big G. I've even networked with others in my audience to provide guest posts and ads which provide a targeted audience. This once again provides me more freedom and control over what gets advertised, when, where, and for how much on my websites and blogs.

BACKUP & AUTOMATION

I really believe in working smarter and not harder. Some of those ways I practice that is by never having my domains registered at the same place as my web hosting provider. When I was learning about networking and server admin back in college I learned that if one thing goes down and everything goes down with it as a result than that would be considered a, "single point of failure". You want to avoid that in your business and besides while I recommend Hostgator as a reliable web hosting provider to access all the files, folders, and databases that make up the sites or blogs there are often much more affordable places to register a domain. Many of them even have regular ongoing discounts that make the invest next to nothing.

I recommend Namecheap
http://kayolhope.com/namecheap

You can easily point the domain to your web hosting plan where your website or blog is hosted by getting your name server settings provided by your web hosting provider (also found in most control panels) and entering them inside the settings of your domain name registered settings of where you purchased and registered your domain.

As far as automation some marketers go overboard and it negatively impacts audience growth as it doesn't seem "real" and can effect search rankings if content is automated as it may be seen as not organic. A tool I use to backup and deploy copies of my sites and blogs for rapid development is WPTwin - http://kayolhope.com/wptwin hands down is one of my biggest secret weapons for creating profitable niche sites.

I've also had success building fully automated community sites with curated content around popular interests using a WordPress theme by fellow marketer Cindy Donovan called, Viral Loop 2.0 - http://kayolhope.com/viralloop/

Divi - http://kayolhope.com/divi is one of 87 themes and 3 plugins by Elegant Themes and is available as part of their affordable membership plans. I initially invested in an annual subscription for their developer license in order to quickly create attractive design and the wide range of features including the page builder tool for the purpose of flipping niche sites. Realizing the value I upgraded to the Lifetime Plan before my first renewal. I love not having to worry about reoccurring costs and use the themes on many of my own niche sites.

www.ingramcontent.com/pod-product-compliance
Lightning Source LLC
Chambersburg PA
CBHW070947200526
45161CB00001BA/23